How to write A Book That Works:
Non-Writer's Guide to Writing a Profitable Book in Six simple actionable steps

How to write A Book That Works:
Non-Writer's Guide to Writing a Profitable Book in Six simple actionable steps

MicroMonitor
2017

Copyright © 2017 by MicroMonitor
All rights reserved. This book or any portion thereof may not be reproduced or used in any manner whatsoever without the express written permission of the publisher except for the use of brief quotations in a book review or scholarly journal.
First Printing: 2017
MicroMonitor
Alexandria, Egypt 21311
www.outatime.tech

Dedication

For my parents, my wife, my loving daughters and my brothers.
Thank you. Your love is the fuel of my life.

Contents

Preface
Step One: So why would you want to write a book anyway?
Step Two: How to come up with an elegant idea that works?
Step Three: I know you're Outatime. How to find out more?
Step Four: How to get out of writer's block syndrome?
Step Five: How to write efficiently
Step Six: How and where to start technically?
Final: The Funnel of Life. Back to Making Decisions

Preface

This guide is intentionally designed to be short, concise and right to the point so you can quickly take immediate action towards your dream of publishing your first book.

Remember that by taking those small steps you are going to join the club. That club which unites people from all around the world who share the same dream of not only speaking and thinking but taking actions to change their lives.

I have tried all those tools and strategies listed in this book. They have worked for me and I use them all the time.

Being so simple is what makes these strategies so successful.

You don't need a complicated plan so that you feel overwhelmed while reading and paralyzed to take any step towards it.

I'm just a normal guy who has some message to share with you. I feel in inspired by using my humble knowledge to convince others to start to take steps to change their lives.

I believe that we both you and me share that same passion for having better quality of life through expanding our knowledge. So let's begin our journey of learning.

Draw your future and start to craft your masterpiece.

Don't die with your idea still inside, book it out loud.

Step One: So why would you want to write a book anyway?

"It is not fair to ask of others what you are not willing to do yourself."   *Eleanor Roosevelt*

You probably have an answer to that question. I know you started to read that book, so you gotta have some good reason to read about writing a book. You must have this idea chasing you. You probably had the idea before but just dropped it completely as you might thought it was some hard thing or impossible to do. You may thought it was something only for great writers. You might have heard about some of your friends or acquaintance has done it and the idea became appealing to you again and you thought it might be possible.

I might not know what exactly goes into your mind but I know what made me think about the idea from the first place. Here are some of my reasons for writing books.

Message

You feel that you have a high quality message and experience that you want to deliver to the world. You know that you have got something you might tell someone who feel appreciated and grateful for you to share with him such useful information.

I got that feeling when I first won an international electronic design contest from Renesas back in 2008.

I thought to myself: "Now that I've won this contest, there might be someone on this planet that might find my information I provide useful for him. He might also use this information to turn his life better just as I did."

I felt that I have something useful to share with the world. That's why I started my first blog about embedded systems design.

For me, writing a blog is so wonderful and fun thing to do. But I recently started to turn to publishing books for some reasons.
To get the audience that doesn't read blogs or prefers books over blog posts.

To try something new

To make something that is (for the old world) a long familiar thing – to write a book is more valuable than to post a blog – although you may make profit from your blog as much or more than that you make from you books.

Anyway, I've decided to turn to books to deliver my messages to the audience. I felt that writing a book that delivers those messages might be something valuable that makes me proud of it overtime.

Self-motivation/ Self challenge

When you get a new idea that you hear that voice inside your brain that keeps telling you: "You can do it." You just cannot help yourself stopping that feeling of self-challenge. You find yourself in continuously asking yourself:
"What if I do it?"
"What would happen to me?"
"How would it change my life?"
"Would it really work?"

You can't find answers to all those questions without accepting the challenge. You may be doing it from the motivation that drives you to do it. It's that urge that keeps pushing you day and night.

It's that sound that keeps your mind restless wishing to get up from your bed to work on your new idea. Motivation is a great driving force.

Fame

You might have heard about some people who became famous after publishing their books. To tell you the truth, fame is not so important to me as much as the need for delivering my message the world. The second is much important to me. But some fame wouldn't hurt.

Money

I won't tell you that you will become rich over night after you publish your first book. But self-publishing is a profitable business indeed. Your first book will bring you some side cash. And after you become more focused on self-publishing you can create more books that sum up together to make good cash. Through your carrier as a self-publisher you might write a book that becomes a hit.

Getting ideas out of your mind

I always felt many ideas flying in my mind all the time. Many of them were really useful and creative. I've always wanted to get them out of my mind and bring them to the real world then share them with people who might find them interesting.

Writing my blog was the first step to do this. Then I found writing a book is another useful way to do it.

When I started to do this regularly, my mind became clearer.

You need to continuously get ideas into paper and books to find your true inner self.

Step Two: How to come up with an elegant idea that works?

"Where focus goes energy flows."
Tony Robbins

Finding idea for your book might be a challenging task for you to begin with. But this is the most important step to make.

It actually determines how successful your book will be and also how you are going to write it. Here are some tips.

Read other books

It's no secret that writing comes after reading. It's said that as a rule if thumb; to write one book you need to read at least ten books first.

You may think writing is rare gift for talented group of people, but if you start to read enough you can find your knowledge has increased to enable you to achieve things you never thought were possible.

Find what you love most

Ask yourself about what you love to write about and what you are good at. It's not about the style or words. It's about the message, experience and information you deliver to your audience.

Write down your ideas to explore yourself

You probably have this urge to start writing your own book but you might not have a clear idea or title to write about.

One of the best ways to overcome this is to start recording your ideas in any form. Try Audio recording, write on keyboard, write on paper or write on sticky notes to get ideas as much as you can. Then you collect them all to one big pile and start to read them all. You'll be amazed by results you get using this strategy.

Search for profitable subjects

You need to know what other people are looking for. You may have a broad idea about your book. Just a big frame only. But considering people needs related to your specialty gives you clear vision and solid ground to stand on.

Search for related books

Try to do some research on large self-publishing market place.

Searching Amazon and Lulu has been a great help for me to get insight for:

Book titles related to my subject,
Book sizes,
Actual book prices,
Book reviews and publicity

Just like any market place, ebooks has large number of customers and users that pay for services and products they are buying and expect they get what they pay for.
You can think if it as a market research.

Do your homework and get brilliant insights of how your dream project is going to look like on that website you are publishing on.

Make physical activity

Yes. You can get your best ideas when you practice physical activity like jogging or power walking. I tried this myself and it works for me like clock work. I actually get most of my best ideas of books or blog posts during running.

What's important is that you focus on your ideas coming on your mind during running or walking and start recording them soon after you get to a journal or a computer keyboard. Remember that great ideas don't stay there too long. You've to capture them quickly. Otherwise, you'll have to make effort trying to remember them. And you may don't.

Write about your trip

People love to know about new places. They would like to hear your story in your trip. It can help them if they travel to that same destination. Traveling has always been an inspiring material for books.

Try Google keyword

Google keyword tool is one of the best tools to find a good book title related to your idea. It's no doubt book title is an important factor for good book sales.

Step Three: I know you're Outatime. How to find out more?

"Time is what we want most, but... what we use worst."   William Penn

Now you know why to write, what to write and how to write it. Here comes a very important question: when to write?

How can I find suitable time through my daily life to write a book that I've always dreamed of writing?

I feel your problem. I have a full time job and a father if two wonderful girls. Here are some tips I've tired and they worked for me.

Early morning writing

You can really write at any free time of the day. But according to many authors and according to my personal experience getting up earlier in the morning and starting to write makes the whole process more time efficient. Silent atmosphere and clarity of your mind makes ideas jump into your head and your productivity rate goes to the maximum.

You can write in the morning what you can write in any other time of the day in doubled time.

Write in small chunks

As you use the method of analyzing your book into small pieces if chapter, subchapters and basic ideas, you can quickly write about any basic idea if them because you've got them already written down as titles.

Those small ideas take short time to write but sum up to make chapters and they quickly made an awesome book.

Use modern tools along with traditional methods

I usually write in computer keyboard. Sometimes I use my spare time to write on my mobile phone.

You can't believe how easy and time efficient this method of mobile writing until you try it.

I know. Writing on mobile phones in the past was a hard process even if you write a short *SMS*. But new smart phones have large displays and keyboards with advanced writing capabilities.

Software with word prediction and word count are just few features to mention. When I tried it I found it very easy and a good way to use my spare and travel time on my books.

From time to time I use the old writing method of paper and pen that has its own magic with me. Sometimes you feel that they give you inspiration by their own. Sometimes you feel the urge to write down your ideas using this old way.

So don't resist it. Just do it and be amazed by the way ideas come to you at that time. Use Daily basis. Make that running time your best friend.

Time is the fastest thing passing in the world. You can make its passage to your side. This is done by make your habits synchronized with time.

You can decide to write as little as an hour or even fifteen minutes only on a daily basis. See what you accomplished after a week or a month.

This has the compounding effect of time. This way time passage is your friend.

Challenge yourself

You can't use time efficiently unless you manage it. And you can't manage it unless measure how much time you spend in certain task. Every time you start writing decide and measure how much time you use.

Time is precious. Time is money. Treat it that way.

Just remember every time you start watching TV shows, reading useless emails or checking Facebook status if your friends that you have something more important to do in your time. Use it wisely to become better.

Step Four: How to get out of writer's block syndrome?

"Either write something worth reading or do something worth writing." Benjamin Franklin

Now that you know your idea and determined your book's title, you can start to write into your book. But is it really that simple?

You may know exactly what title you want to write about but cannot actually do.

How can you start to write your book's content?

This is the actual moment of truth to you. Will you start to write or you'll stop at this point?

Of course you want to start writing your book and this is exactly what I'll help you to achieve using those simple methods I've tried and only those worked for me.

Split the task into sub tasks.

If you really are writing book as a one big task, you'll definitely find it a hard or nearly impossible thing to do.

Most people believe that writing books is something that only some talented writers around the world who can do.

Those majority of people don't even try to write some small chapters of their own books or novels while they can stay late at night to write a long report that their boss have asked them to finish.

This is also something because most people are consumers not producers. Most people are followers and not leaders.

Because as you can see that most people cannot use their spare time without being told how to spend that time wisely. But this doesn't apply for you. Because you've just found your dream and have taken serious steps for chasing it.

So, how to make this task appear as exactly as it is?

I remember when I was young at school; the hardest task in the class was to write a short paragraph of 10 or 20 lines. The only hint I've been given from the teacher to do this task is by writing elements of this paragraph first. I must write those elements to cover the whole paragraph.

Then writing five or more lines about each element covers the whole article with enough ideas and written lines.

Your major title or subject you have settled upon should now be split into some chapters that cover this subject as a whole.

Whatever the number of chapters you decide to write, you should make them enough to give clear and efficient message right to the point of your subject.

Start writing this chapter by also splitting it into some basic ideas.

Then you must cover all the ideas into that single chapter until the end. You'll be amazed by the efficiency and simplicity of this idea. I can tell you it works for me very well.

I know this sounds basic, but many people forget this rule sometimes including me. But if you remember and make it a habit for you it will make writing books seems as systematic process for you.

Write into the waste bin

I heard this word once from a professional writer. Think as if your book that you are writing will never be read by anybody and don't have to be perfect as you write because it will end up into the waste bin.

Most of people think that to create something it has to be perfect and that's why they don't even start. Great writers were not born great. Just as any other skill, you must practice it first to reach a good level in it.

But the main problem is this; people don't practice the skills they want to master because of being afraid of failure or not reaching perfection. Then they don't start at all. So they don't practice the skill at all. Then they never master it.

Remember this; whatever you really want to do. Just start doing it and don't look for perfection.

Just start to do the task in front of you even with a quality of 80%. Don't expect to do something that is 100% right from the start.

Just do it and your mind will do the rest.

Mind map your ideas

I've read books about mind mapping from Tony Buzan and always tried this great tool to visualize my ideas and I always end up getting more creative ideas.

Many tools are available out there for creating Mind Maps on the Web. I really prefer the paper and pen free hand Mind Maps. They make me feel more creative and free to make my own ideas. I really love to draw and to use doodles or cartoons to visualize my ideas and hand drawn Mind Maps makes perfect tool for me to do so.

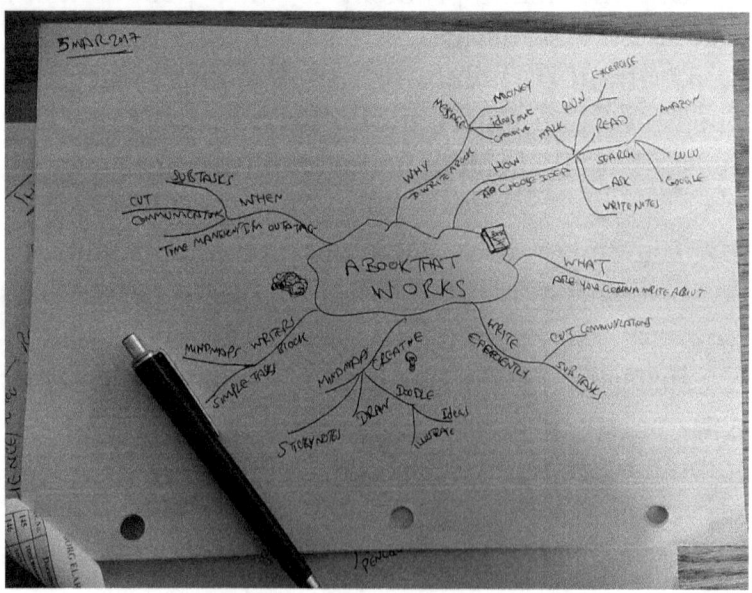

Cut the communications

Again, you need to feel focused in a quiet place that you can work on your keyboard without any distractions. No one to disturb you. No phones. No emails. No internet nor Facebook. Just you, your lovely keyboard, a pencil and a paper.

Step Five: How to write efficiently

"There is nothing to writing. All you do is sitting down at a typewriter and bleed."
Ernest Hemingway

Here are some tips that I've tried myself and it worked for me to write quickly and efficiently.

Write on purpose

Whether you are writing for a book or your blog. All those good targets are legal things you want to achieve to become more productive and have a stream of passive income.

My blogs and book on Amazon was a success that amazed me.

Although I didn't give them so much time and concentration they deserve, but they had unexpected success.

So write with your target in mind.

Your blog, your article, your book. All these targets will make writing easy for you.

Write without editing

Don't look back for editing and correcting words. Just type down your words and ideas before they escape from your mind.

Style, font, spelling, words are all nothing compared to ideas and thoughts. They all can be corrected and adjusted at any time and using automatic methods like word processors on computers and cloud services. But ideas are hard to catch.

Write about a certain subject

You must chose a topic for your article and hence for your book or blog post. Keeping that subject in mind gets your mind focused on that subject and works towards it all the time and helps you achieve it.

Write about a subject you love, know about or deeply willing to learn

It is easier to write about something you already have experience in rather than writing about something you need to get ideas and words about.

You may write about something you have already tried for yourself and succeed – or failed – in it.

You certainly can write about something you love very easily and that is what I advise you to start with.

I remember when I first started my blog I started with something I already love and tried before which is embedded systems and microcontrollers.

You may also start to write about something you don't have great experience in but willing to learn bit by bit and be a lead learner.

You may learn some bit of your subjects and tell your audience about it. Then you start to learn a new bit about the same subject and put it in front of your audience. This helps you learn more efficiently because you are focused on the target about learning for teaching others.

This is also more appealing for your audience because it makes you look so close to them. Especially when you tell your stories about how you learned this piece of information about that subject.

Write without browsing the internet

The internet can really be a huge source for research and information for writing great content and articles. But it can also be s great source of distraction even when you surf some useful things.

That flow of information can be overwhelming.
You can literally be flooded with all this amount of information without doing something useful in your day.

So cut and stop browsing the internet and enjoy getting those good ideas from your mind into the keyboard and to the computer screen.

Write on a good tactile keyboard

I love good keyboards. Tactile keyboards motivate me to write better and feel the buttons under my fingers.

Sometimes I hate writing because of bad keyboards feeling on my finger tips

Do yourself a favor and choose a high quality keyboard. You don't need something fancy or very expensive but you need something ergonomic and comfortable.

Write with the amount of words in mind

I found that when I start with the amount of words predetermined into my mind before writing I become better at writing.

I choose a medium article size to select it about 500 words. When I chose this target I usually get far beyond it about 700 or 800.

Write with time is considered

You must keep in mind that when you challenge your mind he accepts the challenge and challenges you back.

So start with your determination to finish your article after a certain amount of time.

You'll be amazed that your mind can achieve exactly what goals you have challenged him to finish.

What people love from your book?

People not only love the technical part of your story, they also love your story of success. Happiness came to you as you found your passion. Inspire you audience through your words.

Are you having passion for what you do?

Do you love what you are writing about?

If you do people will feel it in every word of your book. So you need to be writing about something you are passionate about and show it to your audience.

People need that inspiration to reach out to the point where they can take immediate action that can change their lives. This is the most beautiful gift you can give to your audience through your book. People always dream of changing to the better life but they don't take action. If you just could do it they are going to love what you do.

Do it with excitement

Feel excited about it and show it. If you are not excited about the book you are writing about you wouldn't be able to complete it to the end. You must have that excitement in every day till you publish it and after that by promoting and marketing it as much as you can.

Useful and inspiring experiments

Do you have done inspiring story to tell it to your audience?

People love what actually works

"What could you do to change your life?"
"What strategy you followed to lose your weight?"
"How could you quit smoking?"
"How could you manage to change your child's bad behavior?"
"How could you build that project?"

Not all inspiring stories are success stories. Some Failure stories are also inspiring. People need to hear you failure story to avoid. People love things that work. If you have a story that can add value to people's lives make sure you include it in your book.

Step Six: How and where to start technically?

How to publish your book? Technical Issues

Now that you've written your book and it is ready to be published. What are going to do?

You should ask yourself: Is it ready to be published?

As we said earlier, you were writing into the waste bin. You were writing without editing your words only to capture your thoughts and ideas before they get away from your head.

Now you should organize your book to make those ideas in a proper readable form for your audience.

1- Chapters must be organized in the right logical order. Spelling check is the first type of test.
2- Check for meaning and integrity of ideas and elements.
3- Formatting and editing of font types and sizes.
4- Illustrations and images to be integrated with words.
5- Blank pages and start of new chapters.

6- Table of contents and links to each chapter/subchapter.
7- Introduction, preface and acknowledgement.

Now it's time for the real publishing online process.

There are many online self-publishing websites that can help you fulfill your dream.

To name a few:
Amazon KDP
Lulu
Nook
And many other self-publishing websites.

Every website has its own terms and conditions you should read carefully to avoid future pitfalls.

You generally can self-publish the same book on many different websites at the same time. But there are some websites or some promotion programs that can have some terms of exclusively publishing the book on that website during that promotion period.

For example, KDP select is a free promotion program by Amazon KDP that makes your book exclusively sold on Amazon Kindle through the promotion period.

It means that if you enroll your book into *Amazon* KDP you cannot self-publish it on *Lulu* during this period of enrollment in KDP select.

So please read terms and conditions carefully.

Final: The Funnel of Life. Back to Making Decisions

In ideal life, we have all the options that we need and have all freedom to choose what to do at any level. Being a little baby makes your life ideal to do anything.

You are not afraid of the consequences of your decisions. You then have the power and ability to virtually make any decision without fear or regret.

When you grow a little bit, you are a little kid. You still can make decisions on your own because your life is still kind of ideal. You are not worrying about making living or economics. You only care about having your candies and having as much joy as you can in your life.

Also being a child makes your ability to become happy very more probable. You can enjoy and appreciate nearly any and everything because you find all things new and exciting.

So you still can make decisions for your ideal life deliberately and not as a reaction.

As you grow older your ability to make decisions not on a reactive basis becomes weaker.

You take decisions of what to do and what to study as reactions to outer options and world events.

You grow older and forget the marvelous ability of making decisions that you were born with. This ability used to be virtually infinite.

Why did you forget this ability then?

Because as you become older your responsibilities grow with you and the less time you have for yourself and the less clarity you have in your mind.

You only take decisions of what to do right now as a reaction to the immediate question you have or has been placed in front of you now.

So how you can reverse this process?

How can you take back your infinite ability to make decisions that are not reactions?

Of course you cannot have back this ability immediately. But you can restore it gradually as you train yourself to make this thing on purpose.

You may think that you are making decisions of your own. But in fact you tend to make decisions on the autopilot system you have used for years.

So the funnel gets narrower as you grow older because you get stuck into many fast going life events and you feel your options getting limited.

You can think of that funnel as a visual representation to opportunities in your life.

If you settle yourself with that narrow funnel it keeps getting narrower.

Tell me when was the last time you made a deliberate decision to do something that is not on a reactive basis?

When was the last time you've decided to start writing a book of your own or even a small article that is not concerned to your daily job or something that you had to?

Tell me when was the last time that you decided to start painting your own masterpiece?

When was the time you decided to take a vacation or go out on a journey with your family without they keep telling you to do so?

But you tell me when was the last time you've decided to start feeling something that you wanted to feel not as a reaction to an outer event on your world?

The problem is that as we grow older, we have more responsibilities and less time. We feel more stressed and busier.

We lose this ideal life that we had as being babies or kids. Then we stop making decisions.
Or we only make daily and immediate decisions as reactions to life events and situations.

The way to make your life better is to start making that funnel wider not narrower as you grow old.

My advice to you if not to settle down and not to sell yourself short.

Respecting yourself starts with your decision to make not actions but first decisions on deliberate basis.

Start now and act immediately. Decisions are like muscles. You must train your decision making muscles right now.

But exactly as the way you start training your muscles slowly and gradually so that they respond to you without being hurt.

You can start training your decision making muscles by making deliberate decisions of something that are completely not reactive to your current situations or life events.

You can start now with your major yet simple and easy decision to make. This decision is to start to make decisions deliberately and consciously as much as you can.

Note that it's not always bad to make decisions on the autopilot or as an immediate reaction to current situations. On the contrary, the faster you can make right and wise decisions the better your life is.

But being always coming from a reactive point of view that is what I call reactive life.

Here is where you should grow your decision making muscles. If you are always making reactive decisions, you are not making decisions at all.

Act now and change your daily life and start building those decision making muscles.

www.ingramcontent.com/pod-product-compliance
Lightning Source LLC
Chambersburg PA
CBHW050248230526
45470CB00005B/2160